50 The Young Chef's Cookbook Recipes

By: Kelly Johnson

Table of Contents

- Easy Homemade Pizza
- Quick Veggie Tacos
- DIY Smoothie Bowls
- Cheesy Garlic Bread
- Chicken Stir-Fry with Rice
- Mini Burger Sliders
- Pasta with Tomato Basil Sauce
- Crispy Veggie Spring Rolls
- Classic Grilled Cheese Sandwich
- Chocolate Chip Pancakes
- Veggie and Hummus Wraps
- Mini Pizzas on English Muffins
- Simple Mac and Cheese
- Fruit and Yogurt Parfaits
- Chicken Quesadillas
- Veggie Frittata
- DIY Breakfast Burritos
- Cinnamon Sugar Toast
- Quick and Easy Guacamole
- Homemade Granola Bars
- Taco Salad
- Easy Pasta Salad
- Baked Sweet Potato Fries
- Veggie Stir-Fry with Noodles
- Chicken Caesar Salad Wraps
- Homemade Pita Chips
- Simple Veggie Fajitas
- Strawberry Banana Smoothies
- Quick Veggie Sauté
- Fruit Kabobs with Yogurt Dip
- Soft Pretzels
- Mini Muffins
- Cheesy Stuffed Mushrooms
- Veggie Nachos
- Spaghetti with Pesto Sauce

- Chocolate-Covered Bananas
- Crispy Baked Chicken Tenders
- Veggie Soup
- Veggie and Cheese Quesadillas
- Sweet and Sour Chicken
- Homemade Pizza Rolls
- Veggie Burger Patties
- Healthy Banana Bread
- Garlic Butter Shrimp
- DIY Sushi Rolls
- Grilled Chicken Skewers
- Mini Breakfast Burritos
- Easy Chocolate Cupcakes
- Avocado Toast with Eggs
- Fruit Smoothie Popsicles

Easy Homemade Pizza

Ingredients

- 1 pizza dough (store-bought or homemade)
- 1/2 cup pizza sauce
- 1 1/2 cups shredded mozzarella cheese
- **Toppings of choice (pepperoni, vegetables, olives, etc.)**

Instructions

1. Preheat your oven to 475°F (245°C).
2. Roll out the pizza dough on a floured surface to your desired thickness.
3. Place the dough on a baking sheet or pizza stone.
4. Spread pizza sauce evenly over the dough.
5. Sprinkle mozzarella cheese on top and add your desired toppings.
6. Bake for 12-15 minutes, or until the crust is golden and the cheese is bubbly.
7. Slice and serve warm.

Quick Veggie Tacos

Ingredients

- 1 can black beans, drained and rinsed
- 1 cup corn kernels
- 1 bell pepper, diced
- 1 avocado, sliced
- 1 tsp cumin
- 1 tsp chili powder
- 8 small flour tortillas
- Salsa and sour cream (optional)

Instructions

1. Heat a pan over medium heat. Add black beans, corn, bell pepper, cumin, and chili powder. Cook for 5-7 minutes until heated through.
2. Warm the tortillas in a separate pan for about 30 seconds on each side.
3. Assemble the tacos by spooning the veggie mixture onto the tortillas.
4. Top with avocado slices, salsa, and sour cream, if desired.
5. Serve warm.

DIY Smoothie Bowls

Ingredients

- 1 cup frozen berries (strawberries, blueberries, etc.)
- 1/2 banana
- 1/2 cup Greek yogurt
- 1/4 cup almond milk or any milk of choice
- Toppings: granola, fresh fruit, chia seeds, coconut flakes

Instructions

1. In a blender, combine frozen berries, banana, Greek yogurt, and almond milk.
2. Blend until smooth, adding more milk if needed for desired consistency.
3. Pour the smoothie into a bowl and top with granola, fresh fruit, chia seeds, and coconut flakes.
4. Serve immediately.

Cheesy Garlic Bread

Ingredients

- 1 loaf French bread
- 1/2 cup unsalted butter, softened
- 2 cloves garlic, minced
- 1 1/2 cups shredded mozzarella cheese
- 1/2 cup grated Parmesan cheese
- 1 tbsp chopped parsley

Instructions

1. Preheat your oven to 375°F (190°C).
2. Slice the French bread in half lengthwise.
3. In a small bowl, combine softened butter, garlic, and parsley. Spread this mixture evenly on both halves of the bread.
4. Sprinkle mozzarella and Parmesan cheeses over the buttered bread.
5. Bake for 10-12 minutes, or until the cheese is melted and bubbly.
6. Slice and serve warm.

Chicken Stir-Fry with Rice

Ingredients

- 2 chicken breasts, sliced thin
- 2 cups mixed vegetables (carrots, bell peppers, broccoli, etc.)
- 2 tbsp soy sauce
- 1 tbsp sesame oil
- 2 cups cooked rice
- 1 tsp ginger, minced
- 1 tsp garlic, minced

Instructions

1. Heat sesame oil in a large skillet over medium-high heat. Add chicken slices and cook until browned, about 5-7 minutes.
2. Add the vegetables, ginger, and garlic to the pan and cook for an additional 3-5 minutes, until the vegetables are tender.
3. Stir in the soy sauce and cooked rice.
4. Cook for another 2-3 minutes, mixing everything well.
5. Serve warm.

Mini Burger Sliders

Ingredients

- 1 lb ground beef
- 1/4 cup breadcrumbs
- 1 egg
- 1 tsp garlic powder
- Salt and pepper to taste
- 12 slider buns
- Cheese slices (optional)
- Toppings: lettuce, tomato, pickles, ketchup, mustard

Instructions

1. Preheat a grill or skillet over medium-high heat.
2. In a bowl, combine ground beef, breadcrumbs, egg, garlic powder, salt, and pepper.
3. Form the mixture into small slider patties.
4. Cook the patties on the grill or skillet for 3-4 minutes on each side, or until cooked to your desired doneness.
5. Toast the slider buns lightly.
6. Assemble the sliders with cheese, lettuce, tomato, pickles, and your preferred condiments.
7. Serve warm.

Pasta with Tomato Basil Sauce

Ingredients

- 8 oz pasta (spaghetti, penne, etc.)
- 2 cups tomato sauce
- 2 cloves garlic, minced
- 1/4 cup fresh basil, chopped
- 1 tbsp olive oil
- Salt and pepper to taste
- Parmesan cheese for serving (optional)

Instructions

1. Cook the pasta according to package instructions.
2. While the pasta cooks, heat olive oil in a pan over medium heat. Add garlic and sauté for 1-2 minutes.
3. Add tomato sauce to the pan and simmer for 5 minutes.
4. Stir in fresh basil and season with salt and pepper.
5. Toss the cooked pasta with the sauce and serve with Parmesan cheese, if desired.

Crispy Veggie Spring Rolls

Ingredients

- 1 cup shredded cabbage
- 1/2 cup shredded carrots
- 1/4 cup green onions, chopped
- 8 rice paper wrappers
- 2 tbsp soy sauce
- 1 tsp sesame oil

Instructions

1. In a bowl, combine cabbage, carrots, and green onions.
2. Dip each rice paper wrapper in warm water for 10-15 seconds until soft.
3. Place a small amount of the veggie mixture in the center of the wrapper and roll tightly, folding in the edges as you go.
4. Heat sesame oil in a pan over medium heat. Fry the spring rolls for 2-3 minutes on each side until golden and crispy.
5. Serve with soy sauce for dipping.

Classic Grilled Cheese Sandwich

Ingredients

- 2 slices bread
- 2 tbsp butter
- 2 slices cheese (American, cheddar, etc.)

Instructions

1. Heat a skillet over medium heat.
2. Butter one side of each slice of bread.
3. Place one slice of bread butter-side down in the skillet. Top with cheese and the other slice of bread, butter-side up.
4. Grill for 2-3 minutes on each side, until golden brown and the cheese is melted.
5. Slice and serve warm.

Chocolate Chip Pancakes

Ingredients

- 1 cup all-purpose flour
- 1 tbsp sugar
- 1 tsp baking powder
- 1/2 tsp baking soda
- 1/2 tsp salt
- 1 cup buttermilk
- 1 egg
- 2 tbsp melted butter
- 1/2 cup chocolate chips

Instructions

1. In a bowl, whisk together flour, sugar, baking powder, baking soda, and salt.
2. In another bowl, combine buttermilk, egg, and melted butter.
3. Pour the wet ingredients into the dry ingredients and stir until just combined.
4. Fold in chocolate chips.
5. Heat a skillet over medium heat and lightly grease it. Pour 1/4 cup of batter onto the skillet for each pancake.
6. Cook for 2-3 minutes on each side, until golden brown. Serve warm with syrup.

Veggie and Hummus Wraps

Ingredients

- 4 large whole wheat tortillas
- 1 cup hummus
- 1 cucumber, thinly sliced
- 1 carrot, shredded
- 1 bell pepper, sliced
- 1/2 avocado, sliced
- Handful of spinach or lettuce

Instructions

1. Lay the tortillas flat on a clean surface.
2. Spread hummus evenly across the center of each tortilla.
3. Layer the cucumber, carrot, bell pepper, avocado, and spinach on top of the hummus.
4. Fold the sides of the tortilla inward and roll tightly.
5. Slice the wraps in half and serve.

Mini Pizzas on English Muffins

Ingredients

- 4 English muffins, split in half
- 1/2 cup pizza sauce
- 1 1/2 cups shredded mozzarella cheese
- Toppings of choice (pepperoni, veggies, olives, etc.)

Instructions

1. Preheat your oven to 375°F (190°C).
2. Place the English muffin halves on a baking sheet.
3. Spread a thin layer of pizza sauce on each half.
4. Top with mozzarella cheese and your preferred toppings.
5. Bake for 10-12 minutes, or until the cheese is melted and bubbly.
6. Slice and serve warm.

Simple Mac and Cheese

Ingredients

- 8 oz elbow macaroni
- 2 tbsp butter
- 2 tbsp all-purpose flour
- 2 cups milk
- 2 cups shredded cheddar cheese
- Salt and pepper to taste

Instructions

1. Cook the macaroni according to package instructions. Drain and set aside.
2. In a large pan, melt butter over medium heat. Stir in flour and cook for 1-2 minutes.
3. Slowly add the milk while whisking, and cook until the sauce thickens.
4. Stir in the shredded cheese until melted and smooth.
5. Add the cooked macaroni to the sauce and stir to combine.
6. Season with salt and pepper to taste, and serve.

Fruit and Yogurt Parfaits

Ingredients

- 1 cup Greek yogurt
- 1 cup mixed fresh fruit (berries, banana, mango, etc.)
- 1/4 cup granola
- 1 tbsp honey (optional)

Instructions

1. In a glass or bowl, layer Greek yogurt, fresh fruit, and granola.
2. Repeat the layers as needed.
3. Drizzle with honey if desired.
4. Serve immediately or refrigerate until ready to eat.

Chicken Quesadillas

Ingredients

- 2 cups cooked chicken, shredded
- 1 cup shredded cheese (cheddar or Mexican blend)
- 4 flour tortillas
- 1/2 cup salsa
- 1 tbsp olive oil

Instructions

1. Heat a skillet over medium heat and add olive oil.
2. Place one tortilla in the skillet and sprinkle with cheese and shredded chicken.
3. Add a spoonful of salsa on top and cover with another tortilla.
4. Cook for 2-3 minutes on each side until golden and crispy.
5. Slice into wedges and serve with extra salsa or sour cream.

Veggie Frittata

Ingredients

- 6 large eggs
- 1/2 cup milk
- 1/2 cup diced bell pepper
- 1/2 cup diced onion
- 1/2 cup spinach, chopped
- 1/2 cup shredded cheese
- Salt and pepper to taste

Instructions

1. Preheat the oven to 375°F (190°C).
2. In a bowl, whisk together eggs, milk, salt, and pepper.
3. Stir in the bell pepper, onion, spinach, and cheese.
4. Pour the mixture into a greased oven-safe skillet.
5. Bake for 20-25 minutes, or until the eggs are set and the top is lightly golden.
6. Slice and serve warm.

DIY Breakfast Burritos

Ingredients

- 4 large flour tortillas
- 4 eggs, scrambled
- 1/2 cup shredded cheese
- 1/2 cup cooked breakfast sausage or bacon (optional)
- 1/2 cup salsa
- 1/4 cup sour cream (optional)

Instructions

1. Warm the tortillas in a pan or microwave.
2. Scramble the eggs in a skillet over medium heat.
3. Lay the warm tortillas flat and fill each with scrambled eggs, cheese, sausage (if using), salsa, and sour cream.
4. Roll up the tortillas tightly and serve immediately.

Cinnamon Sugar Toast

Ingredients

- 4 slices bread
- 2 tbsp butter, softened
- 2 tbsp sugar
- 1 tsp cinnamon

Instructions

1. Preheat the oven to 375°F (190°C).
2. Spread butter on one side of each slice of bread.
3. In a small bowl, mix sugar and cinnamon together.
4. Sprinkle the cinnamon sugar mixture evenly over the buttered side of the bread.
5. Place the bread on a baking sheet and bake for 8-10 minutes until golden brown.
6. Serve warm.

Quick and Easy Guacamole

Ingredients

- 2 ripe avocados
- 1/2 small onion, finely diced
- 1 small tomato, diced
- 1 tbsp lime juice
- 1 tbsp chopped cilantro
- Salt and pepper to taste

Instructions

1. Cut the avocados in half, remove the pit, and scoop the flesh into a bowl.
2. Mash the avocados with a fork until smooth or chunky, depending on preference.
3. Stir in onion, tomato, lime juice, cilantro, salt, and pepper.
4. Serve with chips or as a topping for tacos.

Homemade Granola Bars

Ingredients

- 2 cups rolled oats
- 1/2 cup honey
- 1/2 cup peanut butter
- 1/4 cup chopped nuts (almonds, walnuts, etc.)
- 1/4 cup dried fruit (raisins, cranberries, etc.)
- 1/2 tsp vanilla extract
- 1/4 tsp salt

Instructions

1. Preheat the oven to 350°F (175°C).
2. In a mixing bowl, combine oats, honey, peanut butter, nuts, dried fruit, vanilla, and salt.
3. Stir until well mixed.
4. Spread the mixture into a baking pan lined with parchment paper.
5. Bake for 10-12 minutes, or until the edges are golden.
6. Let cool before cutting into bars.

Taco Salad

Ingredients

- 1 lb ground beef or chicken
- 1 packet taco seasoning
- 4 cups mixed greens (lettuce, spinach, etc.)
- 1 cup cherry tomatoes, halved
- 1/2 cup shredded cheese
- 1/2 cup black beans, rinsed and drained
- 1/4 cup red onion, thinly sliced
- 1/4 cup salsa
- Tortilla chips, crushed
- Sour cream (optional)

Instructions

1. In a skillet, cook the ground beef or chicken over medium heat. Once cooked through, drain any excess fat.
2. Stir in the taco seasoning and follow the package instructions to prepare.
3. In a large bowl, combine the mixed greens, tomatoes, cheese, black beans, and red onion.
4. Top the salad with the seasoned meat, salsa, crushed tortilla chips, and a dollop of sour cream if desired.
5. Toss gently and serve immediately.

Easy Pasta Salad

Ingredients

- 8 oz pasta (rotini, penne, or your choice)
- 1 cup diced cucumber
- 1/2 cup cherry tomatoes, halved
- 1/4 cup red onion, diced
- 1/4 cup black olives, sliced
- 1/2 cup feta cheese
- 1/4 cup Italian dressing

Instructions

1. Cook the pasta according to the package instructions. Drain and rinse under cold water to cool.
2. In a large bowl, combine the cooled pasta, cucumber, tomatoes, onion, olives, and feta cheese.
3. Toss with Italian dressing until evenly coated.
4. Chill in the refrigerator for at least 30 minutes before serving.

Baked Sweet Potato Fries

Ingredients

- 2 large sweet potatoes, peeled and cut into fries
- 2 tbsp olive oil
- 1 tsp garlic powder
- 1/2 tsp paprika
- Salt and pepper to taste

Instructions

1. Preheat the oven to 425°F (220°C).
2. Toss the sweet potato fries with olive oil, garlic powder, paprika, salt, and pepper.
3. Spread the fries in a single layer on a baking sheet.
4. Bake for 25-30 minutes, flipping halfway through, until crispy and golden.
5. Serve hot with ketchup or your favorite dipping sauce.

Veggie Stir-Fry with Noodles

Ingredients

- 8 oz noodles (rice noodles, soba, or your choice)
- 1 tbsp sesame oil
- 1/2 cup bell peppers, sliced
- 1/2 cup broccoli florets
- 1/4 cup carrots, julienned
- 1/4 cup snow peas
- 2 tbsp soy sauce
- 1 tbsp hoisin sauce (optional)
- 1/2 tsp ginger, minced
- 1/2 tsp garlic, minced

Instructions

1. Cook the noodles according to package instructions. Drain and set aside.
2. Heat sesame oil in a large skillet or wok over medium-high heat.
3. Add the bell peppers, broccoli, carrots, and snow peas. Stir-fry for 4-5 minutes until the vegetables are tender-crisp.
4. Add the ginger, garlic, soy sauce, and hoisin sauce, and stir to coat.
5. Add the cooked noodles to the pan and toss everything together until well mixed.
6. Serve immediately.

Chicken Caesar Salad Wraps

Ingredients

- 2 cups cooked chicken, shredded
- 4 large whole wheat tortillas
- 1 cup romaine lettuce, chopped
- 1/2 cup Caesar dressing
- 1/4 cup shredded Parmesan cheese
- Croutons (optional)

Instructions

1. In a large bowl, toss the shredded chicken, lettuce, Caesar dressing, and Parmesan cheese.
2. Lay the tortillas flat on a clean surface and divide the chicken mixture evenly between them.
3. If desired, add croutons for crunch.
4. Roll the tortillas into wraps, folding in the sides as you go.
5. Slice in half and serve.

Homemade Pita Chips

Ingredients

- 4 pita breads, cut into triangles
- 2 tbsp olive oil
- 1 tsp garlic powder
- 1/2 tsp paprika
- Salt to taste

Instructions

1. Preheat the oven to 400°F (200°C).
2. Cut the pita breads into triangles and arrange them in a single layer on a baking sheet.
3. Drizzle with olive oil and sprinkle with garlic powder, paprika, and salt.
4. Bake for 8-10 minutes, or until the chips are golden and crispy.
5. Serve with hummus or your favorite dip.

Simple Veggie Fajitas

Ingredients

- 1 tbsp olive oil
- 1 red bell pepper, sliced
- 1 yellow bell pepper, sliced
- 1 onion, sliced
- 1 zucchini, sliced
- 1 tsp chili powder
- 1/2 tsp cumin
- 1/2 tsp garlic powder
- Salt and pepper to taste
- 4 small flour tortillas
- Sour cream (optional)

Instructions

1. Heat olive oil in a large skillet over medium heat.
2. Add the bell peppers, onion, and zucchini. Cook for 5-7 minutes, stirring occasionally.
3. Sprinkle with chili powder, cumin, garlic powder, salt, and pepper. Stir to coat evenly.
4. Warm the tortillas in a dry skillet or microwave.
5. Serve the veggie mixture in the tortillas with a dollop of sour cream if desired.

Strawberry Banana Smoothies

Ingredients

- 1 cup frozen strawberries
- 1 banana, sliced
- 1/2 cup yogurt (Greek or regular)
- 1/2 cup milk (or almond milk)
- 1 tbsp honey (optional)

Instructions

1. Add the strawberries, banana, yogurt, milk, and honey (if using) to a blender.
2. Blend until smooth and creamy.
3. Pour into glasses and serve immediately.

Quick Veggie Sauté

Ingredients

- 1 tbsp olive oil
- 1 cup broccoli florets
- 1/2 cup bell peppers, sliced
- 1/2 cup zucchini, sliced
- 1/4 cup soy sauce
- 1/2 tsp garlic powder
- Salt and pepper to taste

Instructions

1. Heat olive oil in a large skillet over medium-high heat.
2. Add the broccoli, bell peppers, and zucchini. Sauté for 5-7 minutes, stirring occasionally.
3. Add soy sauce, garlic powder, salt, and pepper, and stir to combine.
4. Continue to sauté for another 2-3 minutes, then serve.

Fruit Kabobs with Yogurt Dip

Ingredients

- 1 cup strawberries, hulled
- 1 cup pineapple chunks
- 1 cup grapes
- 1 banana, sliced
- 1/2 cup Greek yogurt
- 1 tbsp honey
- 1/2 tsp vanilla extract

Instructions

1. Thread the fruit onto wooden or metal skewers, alternating the types of fruit.
2. In a small bowl, mix the Greek yogurt, honey, and vanilla extract.
3. Serve the fruit kabobs with the yogurt dip on the side.

Soft Pretzels

Ingredients

- 1 1/2 cups warm water
- 1 packet active dry yeast (2 1/4 tsp)
- 1 tsp sugar
- 4 cups all-purpose flour
- 1 1/2 tsp salt
- 2 tbsp melted butter
- 1/4 cup baking soda
- 1 egg, beaten (for brushing)
- Coarse salt (for topping)

Instructions

1. In a bowl, combine warm water, yeast, and sugar. Let it sit for 5 minutes until frothy.
2. In a separate bowl, mix the flour and salt. Add the yeast mixture and melted butter. Stir until combined, then knead the dough on a floured surface for about 5-7 minutes until smooth.
3. Place the dough in a greased bowl, cover with a cloth, and let rise for 1 hour, or until doubled in size.
4. Preheat the oven to 450°F (230°C).
5. Punch down the dough and divide it into 8 pieces. Roll each piece into a long rope and form into pretzel shapes.
6. Bring a pot of water to a boil and add the baking soda. Carefully dip each pretzel into the water for 30 seconds, then place on a baking sheet.
7. Brush each pretzel with the beaten egg and sprinkle with coarse salt.
8. Bake for 12-15 minutes until golden brown. Serve warm.

Mini Muffins

Ingredients

- 1 1/2 cups all-purpose flour
- 1/2 cup sugar
- 1 1/2 tsp baking powder
- 1/2 tsp baking soda
- 1/4 tsp salt
- 1/2 cup milk
- 1/4 cup melted butter
- 1 egg
- 1 tsp vanilla extract
- 1/2 cup chocolate chips or fruit (optional)

Instructions

1. Preheat the oven to 350°F (175°C). Grease or line a mini muffin tin with paper liners.
2. In a large bowl, whisk together the flour, sugar, baking powder, baking soda, and salt.
3. In another bowl, mix the milk, melted butter, egg, and vanilla extract.
4. Add the wet ingredients to the dry ingredients and stir until just combined. If using, fold in chocolate chips or fruit.
5. Spoon the batter into the muffin tin, filling each cup about 3/4 full.
6. Bake for 10-12 minutes, or until a toothpick inserted into the center comes out clean. Cool slightly before serving.

Cheesy Stuffed Mushrooms

Ingredients

- 12 large mushroom caps
- 1/2 cup cream cheese, softened
- 1/2 cup shredded mozzarella cheese
- 1/4 cup grated Parmesan cheese
- 1 clove garlic, minced
- 1 tbsp chopped parsley
- Salt and pepper to taste

Instructions

1. Preheat the oven to 375°F (190°C).
2. Remove the stems from the mushrooms and set aside the caps.
3. In a bowl, combine the cream cheese, mozzarella, Parmesan, garlic, parsley, salt, and pepper.
4. Spoon the cheese mixture into the mushroom caps.
5. Arrange the stuffed mushrooms on a baking sheet and bake for 15-20 minutes, or until the mushrooms are tender and the cheese is bubbly. Serve warm.

Veggie Nachos

Ingredients

- Tortilla chips
- 1 cup shredded cheddar cheese
- 1 cup shredded mozzarella cheese
- 1/2 cup black beans, drained and rinsed
- 1/4 cup diced red onion
- 1/2 cup diced bell pepper
- 1/2 cup sliced black olives
- 1/4 cup chopped jalapeños (optional)
- 1/4 cup salsa
- 1/4 cup sour cream
- Guacamole (optional)

Instructions

1. Preheat the oven to 375°F (190°C).
2. Spread a layer of tortilla chips on a baking sheet.
3. Top with shredded cheeses, black beans, red onion, bell pepper, olives, and jalapeños.
4. Bake for 10-12 minutes, or until the cheese is melted and bubbly.
5. Remove from the oven and top with salsa, sour cream, and guacamole. Serve immediately.

Spaghetti with Pesto Sauce

Ingredients

- 8 oz spaghetti
- 1 cup fresh basil leaves
- 2 cloves garlic
- 1/4 cup pine nuts
- 1/2 cup grated Parmesan cheese
- 1/2 cup olive oil
- Salt and pepper to taste

Instructions

1. Cook the spaghetti according to package instructions. Drain, reserving 1/4 cup of pasta water.
2. In a food processor, combine the basil, garlic, pine nuts, and Parmesan. Pulse to combine.
3. With the processor running, slowly add the olive oil and process until smooth.
4. Toss the pesto sauce with the cooked spaghetti, adding the reserved pasta water to help coat the noodles.
5. Season with salt and pepper to taste and serve immediately.

Chocolate-Covered Bananas

Ingredients

- 2 ripe bananas
- 1/2 cup dark or milk chocolate chips
- 1/4 cup chopped nuts (optional)
- 1 tbsp coconut oil (optional)

Instructions

1. Slice the bananas into 1-inch pieces.
2. Melt the chocolate chips (and coconut oil, if using) in a microwave-safe bowl in 30-second intervals, stirring in between.
3. Dip each banana slice into the melted chocolate, then place on a parchment-lined baking sheet.
4. Sprinkle with chopped nuts if desired.
5. Freeze for 1 hour or until the chocolate is set. Serve chilled.

Crispy Baked Chicken Tenders

Ingredients

- 1 lb chicken tenders
- 1 cup breadcrumbs
- 1/2 cup grated Parmesan cheese
- 1 tsp garlic powder
- 1/2 tsp paprika
- Salt and pepper to taste
- 2 eggs, beaten
- 1 tbsp olive oil

Instructions

1. Preheat the oven to 400°F (200°C).
2. In a shallow bowl, combine breadcrumbs, Parmesan, garlic powder, paprika, salt, and pepper.
3. Dip each chicken tender into the beaten eggs, then coat with the breadcrumb mixture.
4. Place the chicken tenders on a baking sheet lined with parchment paper and drizzle with olive oil.
5. Bake for 20-25 minutes, or until golden and crispy. Serve with your favorite dipping sauce.

Veggie Soup

Ingredients

- 1 tbsp olive oil
- 1 onion, diced
- 2 carrots, diced
- 2 celery stalks, diced
- 1 zucchini, diced
- 2 tomatoes, chopped
- 4 cups vegetable broth
- 1 cup spinach
- 1/2 tsp thyme
- Salt and pepper to taste

Instructions

1. Heat olive oil in a large pot over medium heat.
2. Add the onion, carrots, and celery. Cook for 5-7 minutes until softened.
3. Add the zucchini, tomatoes, vegetable broth, and thyme. Bring to a boil, then reduce heat and simmer for 15 minutes.
4. Stir in the spinach and cook for another 5 minutes.
5. Season with salt and pepper to taste and serve warm.

Veggie and Cheese Quesadillas

Ingredients

- 4 flour tortillas
- 1 cup shredded cheese
- 1/2 cup bell peppers, diced
- 1/2 cup corn kernels
- 1/4 cup red onion, diced
- 1/4 cup spinach
- 1 tbsp olive oil

Instructions

1. Heat olive oil in a skillet over medium heat.
2. Add the bell peppers, corn, onion, and spinach. Cook for 3-5 minutes until tender.
3. Remove the veggies from the skillet and set aside.
4. Place a tortilla in the skillet and sprinkle with cheese. Add a layer of veggies and top with another tortilla.
5. Cook for 2-3 minutes per side, until golden brown and the cheese is melted.
6. Slice into wedges and serve.

Sweet and Sour Chicken

Ingredients

- 1 lb chicken breast, cubed
- 1/2 cup cornstarch
- 1/2 cup vegetable oil
- 1/2 cup pineapple chunks
- 1/2 bell pepper, diced
- 1/4 cup vinegar
- 1/4 cup sugar
- 1/4 cup ketchup
- 2 tbsp soy sauce

Instructions

1. Coat the chicken cubes in cornstarch.
2. Heat the oil in a large skillet over medium heat and cook the chicken until golden and cooked through.
3. Remove the chicken and set aside.
4. In the same skillet, add pineapple, bell pepper, vinegar, sugar, ketchup, and soy sauce. Simmer for 3-5 minutes.
5. Return the chicken to the skillet and toss to coat with the sauce.
6. Serve with rice.

Homemade Pizza Rolls

Ingredients

- 1 pizza dough (store-bought or homemade)
- 1/2 cup pizza sauce
- 1 1/2 cups shredded mozzarella cheese
- 1/2 cup pepperoni slices or any other favorite toppings (optional)
- 1 tbsp olive oil
- 1 tsp dried oregano
- 1 tsp garlic powder

Instructions

1. Preheat the oven to 375°F (190°C).
2. Roll out the pizza dough into a rectangle on a lightly floured surface.
3. Spread a thin layer of pizza sauce over the dough.
4. Sprinkle the shredded mozzarella cheese evenly on top, then add any desired toppings.
5. Carefully roll up the dough into a tight log and slice into 1-inch pieces.
6. Place the pizza rolls on a greased baking sheet, brush with olive oil, and sprinkle with oregano and garlic powder.
7. Bake for 12-15 minutes, or until golden brown and the cheese is bubbly. Serve with extra pizza sauce for dipping.

Veggie Burger Patties

Ingredients

- 1 can (15 oz) black beans, drained and mashed
- 1/2 cup breadcrumbs
- 1/4 cup grated carrot
- 1/4 cup finely chopped onion
- 1/4 cup corn kernels
- 1/4 cup chopped spinach
- 1 egg
- 1 tsp garlic powder
- Salt and pepper to taste
- Olive oil for frying

Instructions

1. In a bowl, combine the mashed black beans, breadcrumbs, grated carrot, onion, corn, spinach, and egg.
2. Add garlic powder, salt, and pepper, and mix until everything is well combined.
3. Form the mixture into patties (about 4-6 depending on size).
4. Heat olive oil in a skillet over medium heat and cook the patties for 4-5 minutes per side, until golden and crispy.
5. Serve on burger buns with your favorite toppings.

Healthy Banana Bread

Ingredients

- 2 ripe bananas, mashed
- 1/4 cup honey or maple syrup
- 1/4 cup olive oil or melted coconut oil
- 2 eggs
- 1 tsp vanilla extract
- 1 1/2 cups whole wheat flour
- 1 tsp baking soda
- 1/4 tsp salt
- 1/2 tsp cinnamon
- 1/4 cup chopped walnuts or chocolate chips (optional)

Instructions

1. Preheat the oven to 350°F (175°C) and grease a loaf pan.
2. In a large bowl, mix the mashed bananas, honey (or maple syrup), oil, eggs, and vanilla extract.
3. In another bowl, whisk together the whole wheat flour, baking soda, salt, and cinnamon.
4. Gradually add the dry ingredients to the wet ingredients and stir until combined.
5. If desired, fold in walnuts or chocolate chips.
6. Pour the batter into the loaf pan and bake for 50-60 minutes, or until a toothpick comes out clean. Let cool before slicing.

Garlic Butter Shrimp

Ingredients

- 1 lb shrimp, peeled and deveined
- 4 tbsp butter
- 3 cloves garlic, minced
- 1 tbsp lemon juice
- 1/4 tsp red pepper flakes (optional)
- Salt and pepper to taste
- Chopped parsley for garnish

Instructions

1. Heat butter in a large skillet over medium heat.
2. Add the minced garlic and cook for 1-2 minutes, until fragrant.
3. Add the shrimp, lemon juice, red pepper flakes (if using), salt, and pepper.
4. Cook for 2-3 minutes per side, or until the shrimp are pink and opaque.
5. Garnish with chopped parsley and serve with rice or pasta.

DIY Sushi Rolls

Ingredients

- 2 cups sushi rice, cooked and cooled
- 1/4 cup rice vinegar
- 1 tbsp sugar
- Nori (seaweed) sheets
- 1 cucumber, julienned
- 1 avocado, sliced
- 1/2 lb sushi-grade fish (optional, like tuna or salmon)
- Soy sauce for dipping
- Pickled ginger (optional)

Instructions

1. Mix the rice vinegar and sugar in a small bowl, then stir it into the cooled sushi rice.
2. Lay a sheet of nori on a sushi mat or a clean surface.
3. Spread a thin layer of rice over the nori, leaving a small border at the top.
4. Add cucumber, avocado, and fish (if using) in a row along the center of the rice.
5. Roll the sushi tightly using the mat, then slice into bite-sized pieces.
6. Serve with soy sauce and pickled ginger.

Grilled Chicken Skewers

Ingredients

- 1 lb chicken breast, cut into cubes
- 1/4 cup olive oil
- 2 tbsp soy sauce
- 1 tbsp lemon juice
- 1 tsp garlic powder
- 1 tsp paprika
- Salt and pepper to taste
- Wooden skewers (soaked in water for 30 minutes)

Instructions

1. In a bowl, combine the olive oil, soy sauce, lemon juice, garlic powder, paprika, salt, and pepper.
2. Add the chicken cubes to the marinade and let it sit for at least 30 minutes.
3. Thread the chicken cubes onto the skewers.
4. Preheat the grill to medium-high heat.
5. Grill the skewers for 5-7 minutes per side, or until the chicken is cooked through.
6. Serve with a side of veggies or rice.

Mini Breakfast Burritos

Ingredients

- 4 small flour tortillas
- 4 scrambled eggs
- 1/2 cup shredded cheese
- 1/4 cup diced tomatoes
- 1/4 cup diced bell pepper
- 1/4 cup cooked bacon or sausage (optional)
- Salsa and sour cream for serving

Instructions

1. Scramble the eggs in a skillet over medium heat.
2. Lay a tortilla flat and place a spoonful of scrambled eggs in the center.
3. Add shredded cheese, tomatoes, bell pepper, and bacon or sausage if using.
4. Roll up the tortilla to form a burrito.
5. Serve with salsa and sour cream on the side.

Easy Chocolate Cupcakes

Ingredients

- 1 1/2 cups all-purpose flour
- 1/2 cup cocoa powder
- 1 tsp baking powder
- 1/2 tsp baking soda
- 1/2 tsp salt
- 1 cup sugar
- 1/2 cup vegetable oil
- 2 eggs
- 1 tsp vanilla extract
- 1 cup milk

Instructions

1. Preheat the oven to 350°F (175°C) and line a muffin tin with paper liners.
2. In a bowl, whisk together the flour, cocoa powder, baking powder, baking soda, salt, and sugar.
3. In another bowl, combine the oil, eggs, vanilla, and milk.
4. Add the wet ingredients to the dry ingredients and mix until combined.
5. Spoon the batter into the muffin tin, filling each cup about 2/3 full.
6. Bake for 18-20 minutes, or until a toothpick inserted comes out clean. Cool before frosting.

Avocado Toast with Eggs

Ingredients

- 2 slices bread, toasted
- 1 ripe avocado, mashed
- 2 eggs
- Salt and pepper to taste
- Red pepper flakes (optional)

Instructions

1. Mash the avocado in a bowl and season with salt and pepper.
2. Spread the mashed avocado evenly over the toasted bread.
3. Cook the eggs to your preference (fried, scrambled, or poached).
4. Place the eggs on top of the avocado toast.
5. Sprinkle with red pepper flakes for extra flavor, if desired.

Fruit Smoothie Popsicles

Ingredients

- 1 cup mixed fruit (berries, mango, banana)
- 1/2 cup Greek yogurt or coconut milk
- 1 tbsp honey or maple syrup

Instructions

1. Blend the fruit, yogurt, and honey until smooth.
2. Pour the mixture into popsicle molds.
3. Insert sticks and freeze for 4-6 hours, or until solid.
4. Remove from the molds and enjoy a refreshing, healthy treat!

www.ingramcontent.com/pod-product-compliance
Lightning Source LLC
LaVergne TN
LVHW081506060526
838201LV00056BA/2958